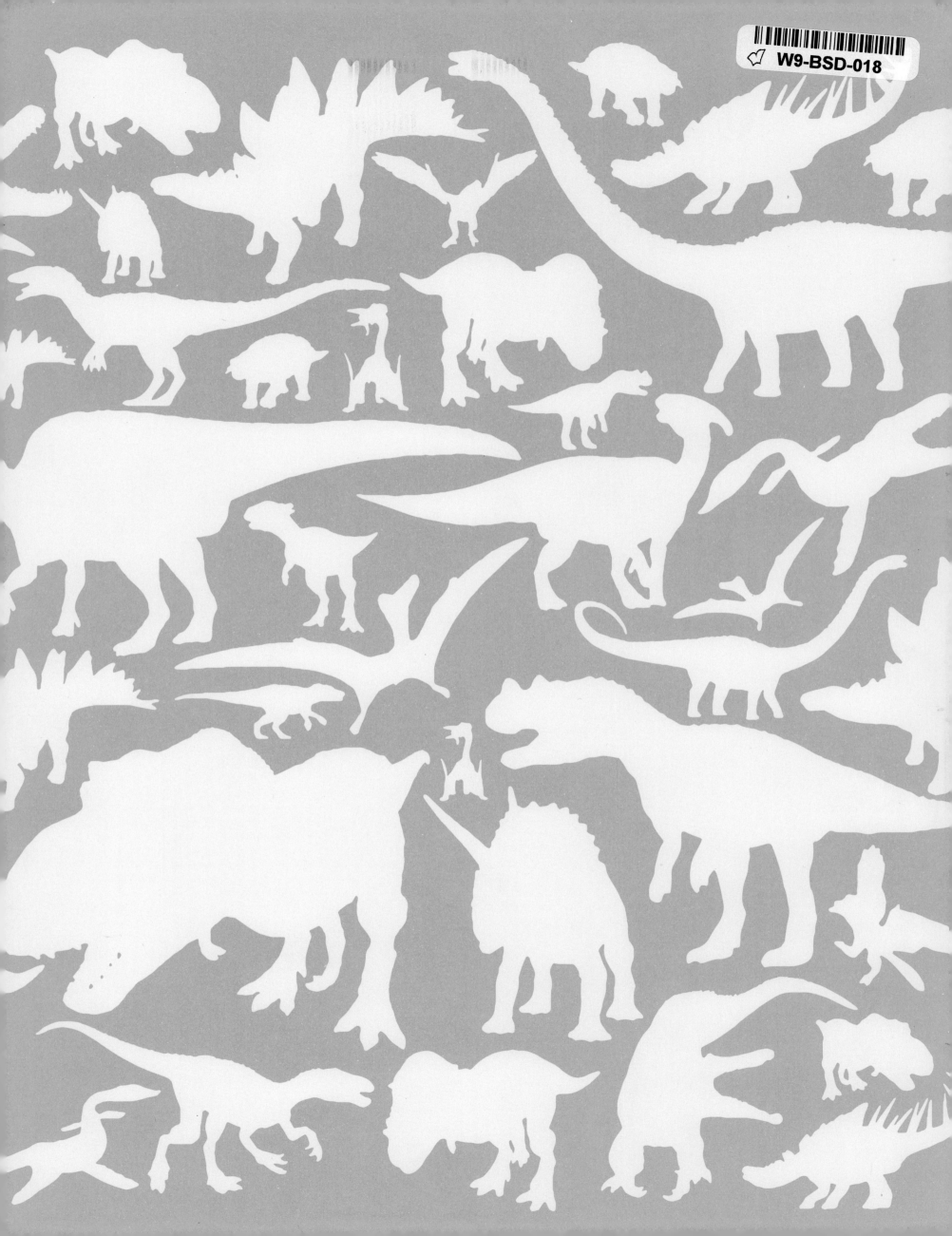

The Big Book of
DINOSAURS

 Penguin Random House

DK UK

Project editor Sam Priddy
Project art editor Fiona Macdonald
Designer Jim Green
US editor Margaret Parrish
Additional illustrators Arran Lewis, Simon Mumford
Senior producer, Pre-production Francesca Wardell
Senior producers Andrew Beehag, Srijana Gurung
Managing editor Laura Gilbert
Managing art editor Diane Peyton Jones
Publisher Sarah Larter
Publishing director Sophie Mitchell

DK India

Senior editor Shatarupa Chaudhuri
Project editor Suneha Dutta
Art editor Shreya Sadhan
Assistant art editor Kartik Gera
DTP designers Bimlesh Tiwary, Jagtar Singh
Managing editor Alka Thakur Hazarika
Senior managing art editor Romi Chakraborty
CTS manager Balwant Singh
Production manager Pankaj Sharma
Picture researcher Sumedha Chopra

Original editor Lara Tankel Holtz
Original designer Mary Sandberg

First American Edition, 1994
This edition published in the United States in 2015 by
DK Publishing, 1450 Broadway, Suite 801, New York, NY 10018

Published in Great Britain by Dorling Kindersley Limited.

A catalog record for this book is available from the Library of Congress.
ISBN 978-1-4654-4377-9

DK books are available at special discounts when purchased in bulk
for sales promotions, premiums, fund-raising, or educational use.
For details, contact: DK Publishing Special Markets,
1450 Broadway, Suite 801, New York, NY 10018
SpecialSales@dk.com

Printed and bound in China

For the curious

www.dk.com

DORLING KINDERSLEY would like to thank Olivia Stanford for proofreading.

The publisher would like to thank the following for their kind permission to reproduce their photographs: (Key: a-above; b-below/bottom; c-centre; f-far; l-left; r-right; t-top)
4-5 Dorling Kindersley: Senckenberg Nature Museum, Frankfurt (bc). **4 Dorling Kindersley:** The American Museum of Natural History (c); Natural History Museum, London (tc, cla); Peter Minister (clb). **6 Dorling Kindersley:** The American Museum of Natural History (tr). **6-7 Dorling Kindersley:** Senckenberg Gesellshaft Fuer Naturforschugn Museum. **11 Dorling Kindersley:** Natural History Museum, London (bl); Royal Tyrrell Museum of Palaeontology, Alberta, Canada (t). **12 Dorling Kindersley:** Royal Tyrrell Museum of Palaeontology, Alberta, Canada (clb). **13 Dorling Kindersley:** Royal Tyrrell Museum of Palaeontology, Alberta, Canada (bl). **Science Photo Library:** Julius T Csotonyi (br). **14 Dorling Kindersley:** Natural History Museum, London (cra). **15 Dorling Kindersley:** Natural History Museum, London (cl); Staatliches Museum fur Naturkunde Stuttgart (tr); Royal Tyrrell Museum of Palaeontology, Alberta, Canada (bl). **16 Getty Images:** Arthur Dorety / Stocktrek Images (br). **18 Dorling Kindersley:** Carnegie Museum of Natural History, Pittsburgh (tr). **23 Dorling Kindersley:** Natural History Museum, London (cl); Senckenberg Nature Museum, Frankfurt (tr). **24 Dorling Kindersley:** Royal Tyrrell Museum of Palaeontology, Alberta, Canada (bl). **26 Dorling Kindersley:** The American Museum of Natural History (tl). **27 Dorling Kindersley:** Royal Tyrrell Museum of Palaeontology, Alberta, Canada (tr). **28 Dorling Kindersley:** Natural History Museum, London (b). **The Natural History Museum, London:** (cl). **29 Corbis:** Sergey Krasovskiy / Stocktrek Images (t). **Dorling Kindersley:** Natural History Museum, London (br).
Cover images: Front: **Dreamstime.com:** Panaceadoll (c/) (Background).

All other images © Dorling Kindersley
For further information see: **www.dkimages.com**

The Big Book of
DINOSAURS

Written by
Angela Wilkes and Darren Naish

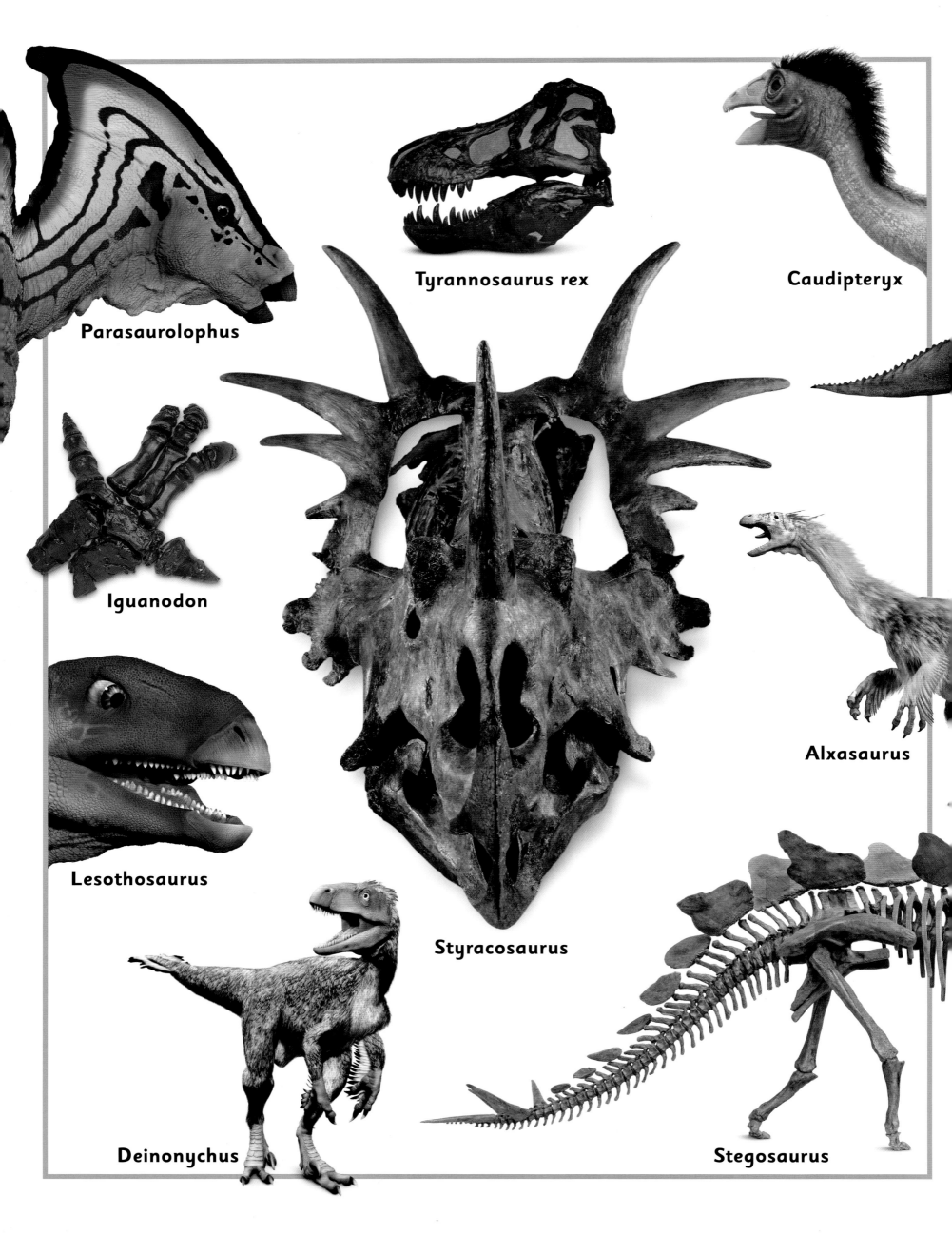

Parasaurolophus

Tyrannosaurus rex

Caudipteryx

Iguanodon

Alxasaurus

Lesothosaurus

Styracosaurus

Deinonychus

Stegosaurus

Contents

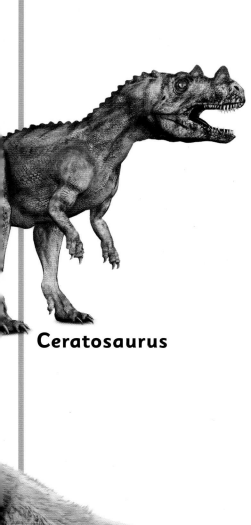

Eoraptor

Ceratosaurus

Triceratops

Saltasaurus

Pachycephalosaurus

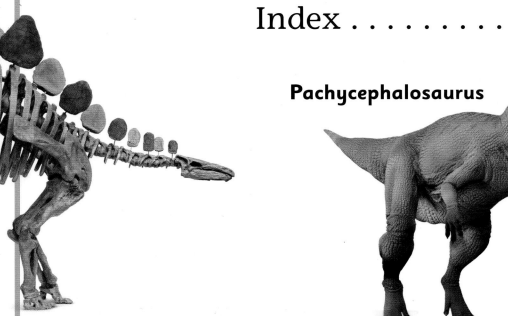

Dinosaur clues

Clues to the past

How do we know so much about dinosaurs when the last ones died millions and millions of years ago? Scientists hunt for the fossil remains of dinosaur bones and teeth, buried in rocks. They use these clues to find out as much as they can about dinosaurs.

This hole shows where the dinosaur's eye was

Tyrannosaurus rex skull

Heavy tail helped to balance the body

Tyrannosaurus rex's huge jaw and sharp teeth show that it was a fierce meat-eater

Tailbones

Strong legs

Rebuilding a dinosaur

Scientists can fit together a dinosaur's fossil bones to build a life-sized skeleton, like the Tyrannosaurus rex here. They usually make models of any bones that are missing.

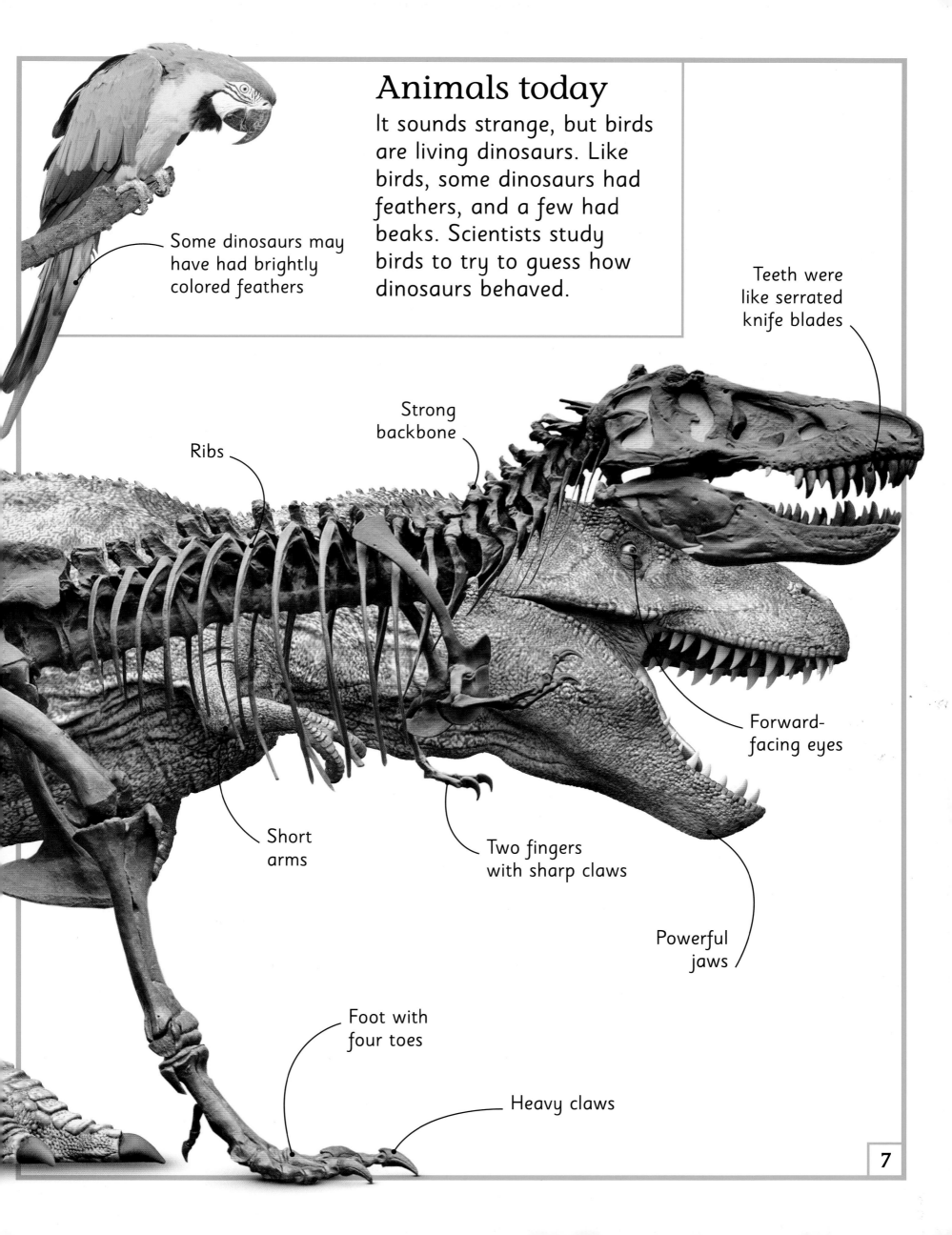

Animals today

It sounds strange, but birds are living dinosaurs. Like birds, some dinosaurs had feathers, and a few had beaks. Scientists study birds to try to guess how dinosaurs behaved.

Some dinosaurs may have had brightly colored feathers

Teeth were like serrated knife blades

Strong backbone

Ribs

Forward-facing eyes

Short arms

Two fingers with sharp claws

Powerful jaws

Foot with four toes

Heavy claws

Hollow crest

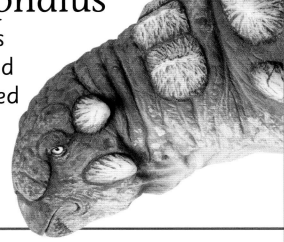

Euoplocephalus

Euoplocephalus was an armored dinosaur covered in bony lumps and bumps.

Corythosaurus

This duck-billed dinosaur had a crest on its head that looked like a plate standing on edge.

Triceratops

This big plant-eater had a head frill and three sharp horns.

Stegosaurus

This plant-eater had two rows of plates along its back and spikes on its tail, which were used for defense.

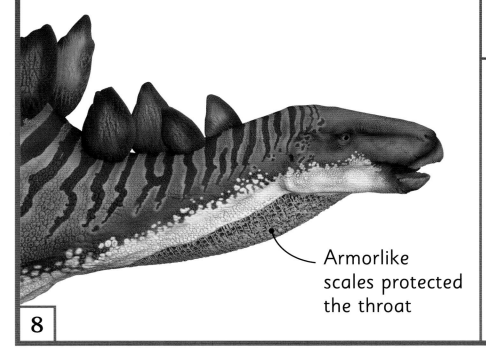

Armorlike scales protected the throat

Citipati

Citipati had a strong, parrotlike beak and a large crest on its head.

Citipati was covered in feathers

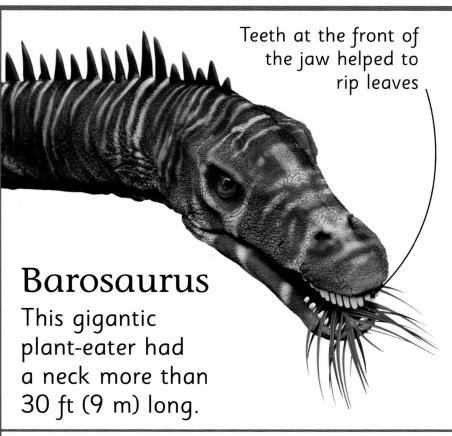

Teeth at the front of the jaw helped to rip leaves

Barosaurus

This gigantic plant-eater had a neck more than 30 ft (9 m) long.

Alxasaurus had a long neck

Alxasaurus

This dinosaur from China was covered in downy feathers.

Edmontonia

Edmontonia had a tough armor of bony plates and fierce spikes, which it used when charging at enemies. It ate mainly moss and ferns.

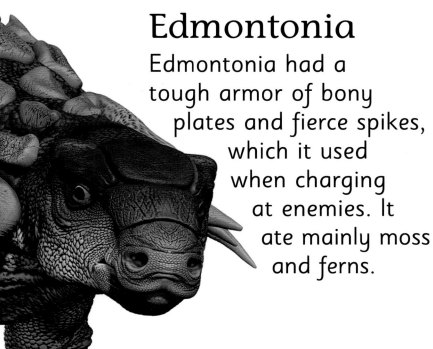

Lesothosaurus

This small and light dinosaur could run very fast, and so could get away from its enemies quickly. It had big eyes, which enabled it to see all around and allowed it to spot danger easily.

Crown of small spikes

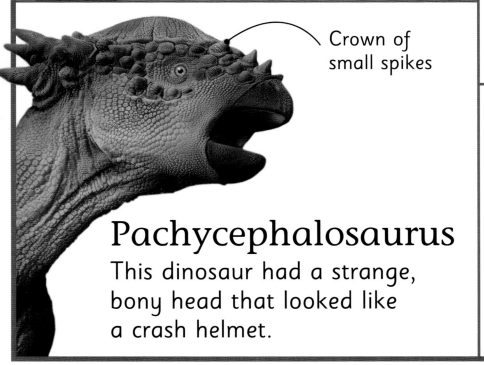

Pachycephalosaurus

This dinosaur had a strange, bony head that looked like a crash helmet.

Iguanodon

Iguanodon was a big, plant-eating dinosaur with lots of strong teeth.

Fast and fierce

Deinonychus

Deinonychus was a fast and very fierce dinosaur. It pinned its victims down on the ground with the long, curved claws on its feet. It used its razor-sharp teeth to tear off chunks of flesh.

Deinonychus had 70 jagged teeth, which helped it to eat tough meat

Flexible, birdlike neck

Troodon's eyes faced forward

Troodon

This quick-witted dinosaur had a brain that was bigger than that of most dinosaurs. Its large eyes helped it to hunt for prey at night.

Its claw was as long as your whole hand

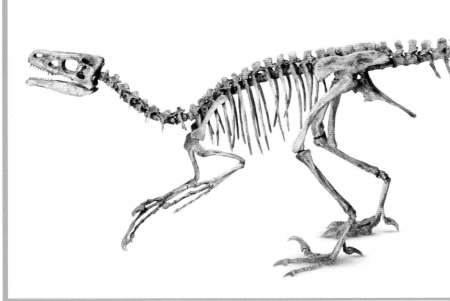

Ornitholestes

Ornitholestes was light and speedy and had a very long tail. It probably hunted small reptiles.

Herrerasaurus used its long tail to stay balanced

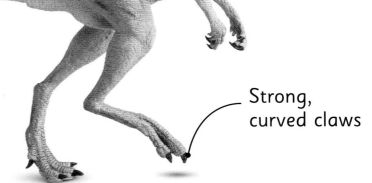

Herrerasaurus

Herrerasaurus was one of the first dinosaurs, living 225 million years ago. It was as long as a small car.

Strong, curved claws

Dromaeosaurus

This dinosaur's name means "running lizard." Dromaeosaurus was an active hunter. Its skull shows that it had powerful jaws lined with saw-edged teeth.

Compsognathus

Compsognathus lived 150 million years ago and was no bigger than a chicken. It could run very swiftly to catch small lizards and insects to eat.

Compsognathus had a narrow head

11

Beaked dinosaurs

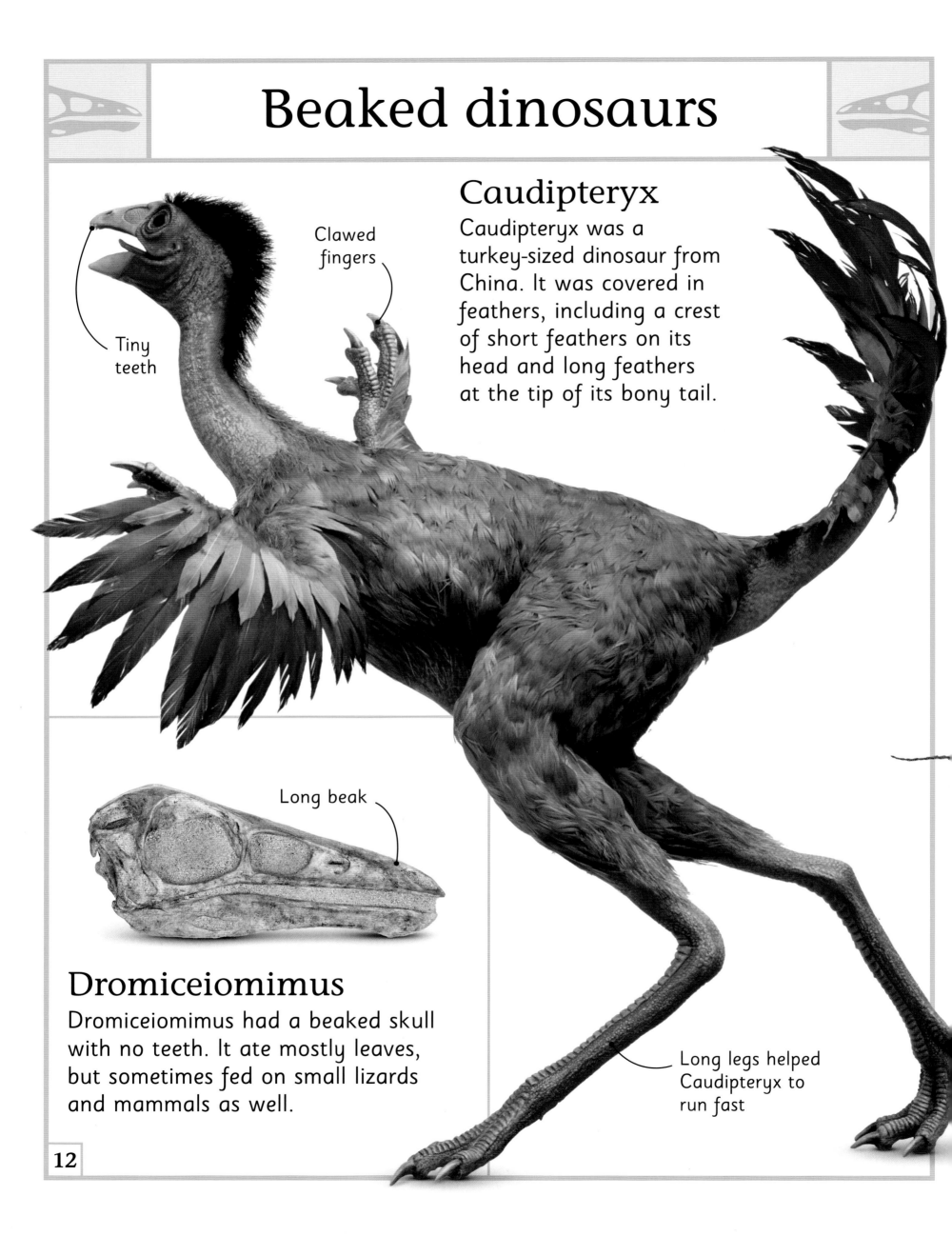

Caudipteryx

Caudipteryx was a turkey-sized dinosaur from China. It was covered in feathers, including a crest of short feathers on its head and long feathers at the tip of its bony tail.

Tiny teeth

Clawed fingers

Long beak

Dromiceiomimus

Dromiceiomimus had a beaked skull with no teeth. It ate mostly leaves, but sometimes fed on small lizards and mammals as well.

Long legs helped Caudipteryx to run fast

Small head with
a toothless beak

Gallimimus

Gallimimus looked like
a big ostrich. It was a fast
runner and could have
kept up with a racehorse.

Long tail helped
Gallimimus to keep its
balance while running

Struthiomimus

Struthiomimus had
three long fingers
with sharp claws,
which were used
to pick at leaves
and fruits.

Despite its
long feathers,
Struthiomimus
couldn't fly

Big toes
with claws

Long,
flexible neck

Shuvuuia

Shuvuuia was the size
of a chicken. Its slender
jaws had tiny teeth and
it probably ate ants
and termites.

Ornithomimus

Ornithomimus was a toothless,
birdlike dinosaur. It had a small head,
a long, thin neck, and a big beak.

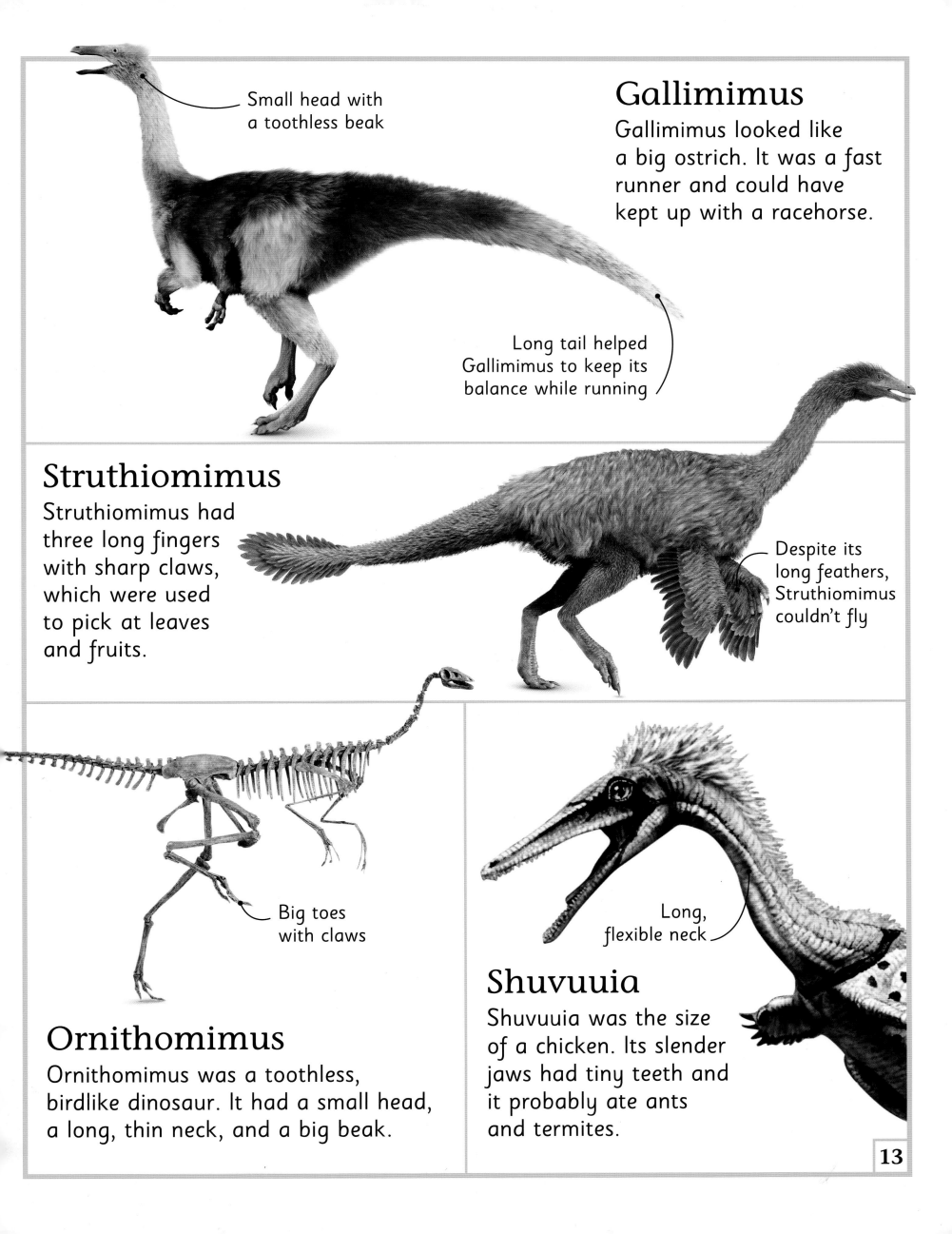

Terrible teeth

Tyrannosaurus rex

Scientists can tell what kind of food an animal eats by looking at its teeth. Tyrannosaurus rex had huge jaws that could open very wide and long, sharp teeth.

Duriavenator

Duriavenator's teeth were curved like daggers. When a tooth broke or wore out, a new one grew in its place.

New tooth ready to come through

These jaws were strong enough to crush bones

Tyrannosaurus rex's teeth were as long as table knives

Allosaurus

Allosaurus was a savage meat-eater. Its teeth were sharp and ideal for slicing through flesh. They curved backward to give Allosaurus a firm grip on its victims.

Bladelike teeth

Diplodocus

Diplodocus was an enormous plant-eater. It had thin teeth, like small pencils, for ripping leaves from branches.

Pointed fangs

Curved teeth tore through flesh

Heterodontosaurus

Heterodontosaurus was a plant-eater. It had a horny beak and teeth for cutting and grinding leaves.

Eoraptor

This little meat-eater had small, sharp teeth. It probably ate lizards and big insects.

Mighty meat-eaters

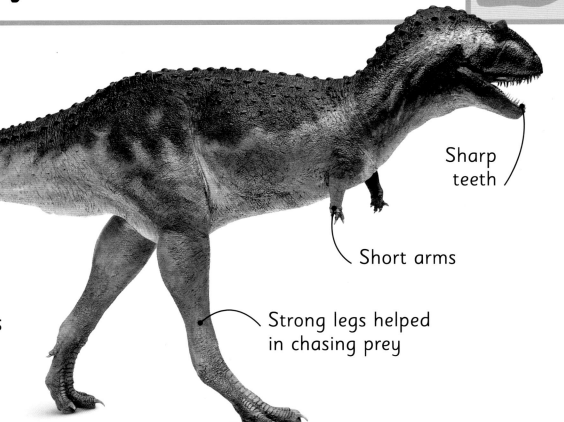

Sharp teeth

Short arms

Strong legs helped in chasing prey

Carnotaurus

The fiercest dinosaurs were the two-legged meat-eaters such as Carnotaurus. It hunted other dinosaurs or ate dead animals that it found.

Massive jaws with rows of fangs

Tyrannosaurus rex

Tyrannosaurus was one of the biggest and strongest meat-eating animals ever— it was nearly as tall as a two-story house. Even though T. rex was very heavy, scientists think it could sprint over short distances.

Acrocanthosaurus

Acrocanthosaurus was a strong predator with knifelike teeth that could tear open tough skin.

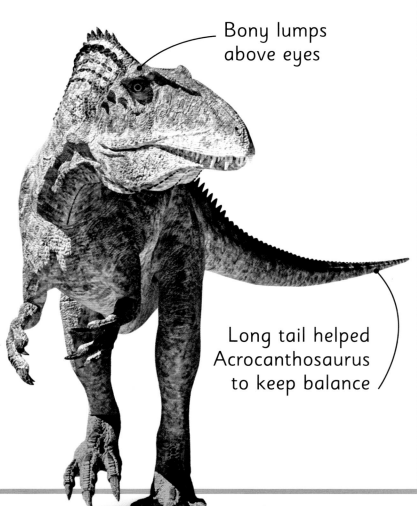

Bony lumps above eyes

Long tail helped Acrocanthosaurus to keep balance

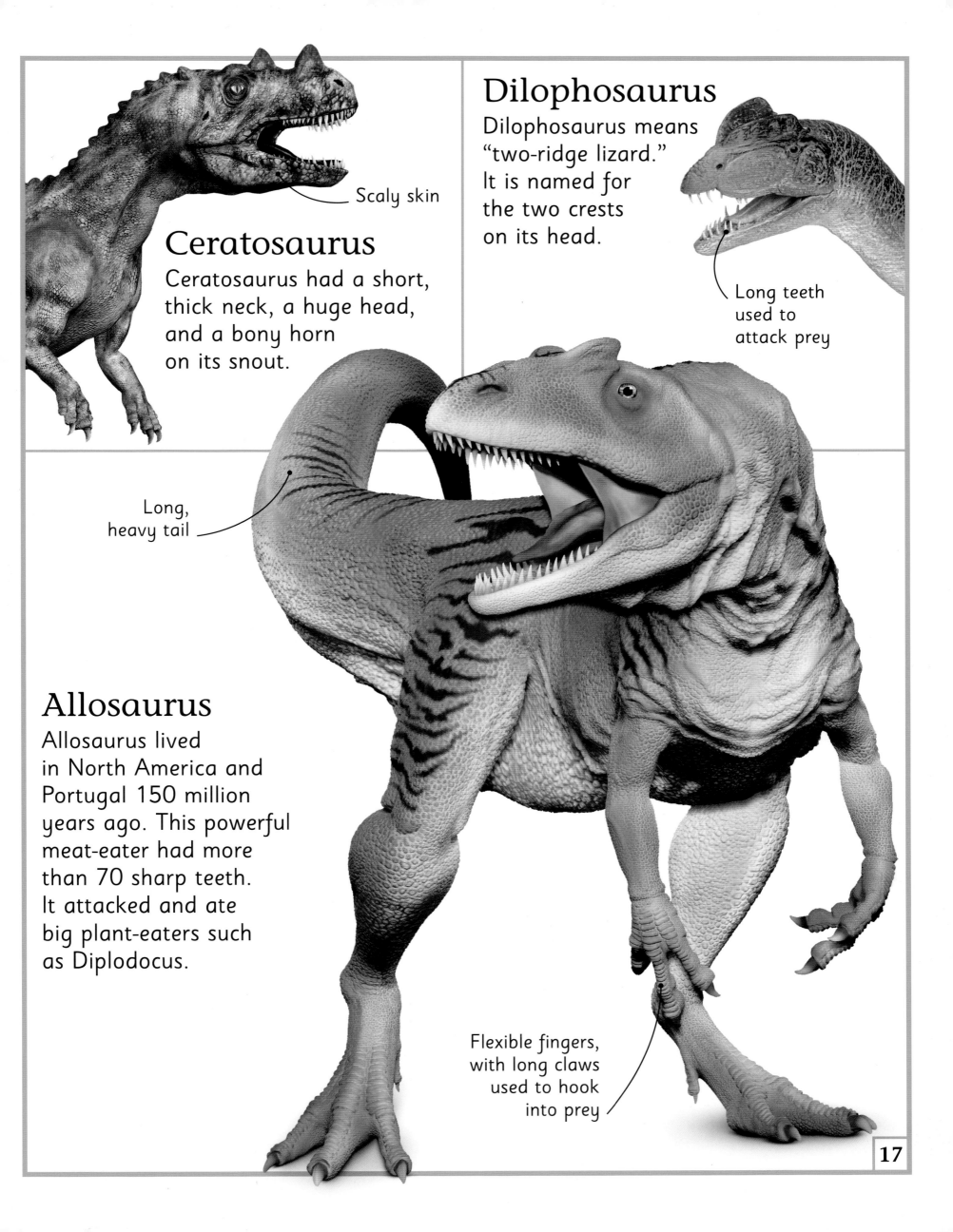

Ceratosaurus

Scaly skin

Ceratosaurus had a short, thick neck, a huge head, and a bony horn on its snout.

Dilophosaurus

Dilophosaurus means "two-ridge lizard." It is named for the two crests on its head.

Long teeth used to attack prey

Long, heavy tail

Allosaurus

Allosaurus lived in North America and Portugal 150 million years ago. This powerful meat-eater had more than 70 sharp teeth. It attacked and ate big plant-eaters such as Diplodocus.

Flexible fingers, with long claws used to hook into prey

Biggest on Earth

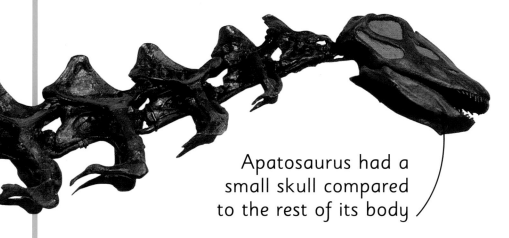

Apatosaurus

This dinosaur used its peglike teeth to strip leaves from plants. Apatosaurus was so big, it probably had to spend most of the day eating.

Apatosaurus had a small skull compared to the rest of its body

Mamenchisaurus

Mamenchisaurus's neck grew up to 50 ft (15 m) long. That's nearly three times as long as a giraffe's neck.

The long, thin tail was carried off the ground

Argentinosaurus

Argentinosaurus was probably the heaviest dinosaur ever found. Scientists think it could have weighed as much as six fire engines.

Tough protective scales

Barosaurus had a strong, whiplike tail

Diplodocus

Diplodocus was the longest dinosaur of all. It was much longer than a tennis court. Despite its massive size, its brain was tiny.

Diplodocus stripped leaves off branches with its long, thin teeth

Saltasaurus

Saltasaurus's back and sides were protected by bony plates and lumps beneath its skin.

Saltasaurus's tough skin made it hard for predators to eat it

Barosaurus's heavy neck was held up by strong bones

Barosaurus

Barosaurus was one of the tallest dinosaurs. It could reach treetops as high as a five-story building.

Armored tanks

Scelidosaurus

Scelidosaurus had rows of ridged bony plates running down its neck, back, and tail.

Short, stocky limbs

Gargoyleosaurus

Gargoyleosaurus had seven teeth at the front of its jaw, which it used to tear leaves and stems off plants.

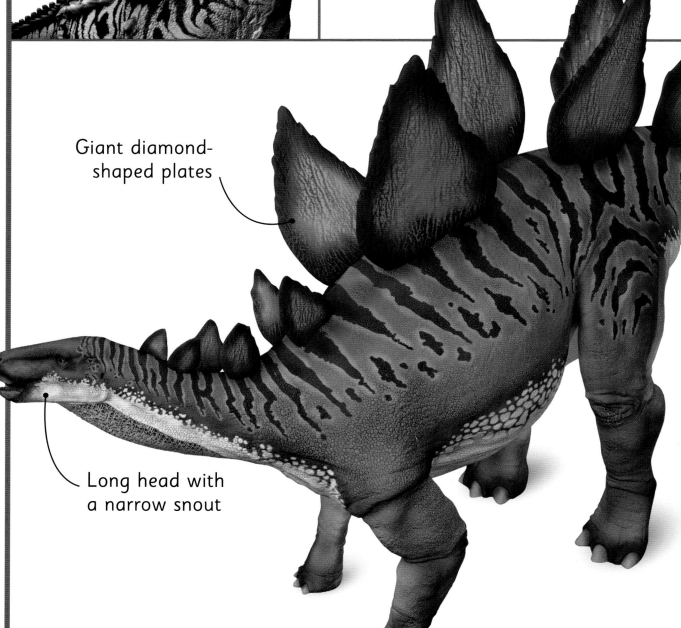

Giant diamond-shaped plates

Sharp tail spikes

Long head with a narrow snout

Stegosaurus

Stegosaurus was the largest of the plated dinosaurs. It probably lashed its spiked tail to defend itself from hungry meat-eaters.

Kentrosaurus

Kentrosaurus had sharp, pointed spikes that ran along its tail. This plant-eater could whip its tail from side to side to injure its attackers.

Spikes grew from the shoulders

Huayangosaurus

This dinosaur had small horns on the top of its head, and a short, broad snout. It ate ferns, leaves, and fruit.

Tall, thin plates lined its back

Sauropelta

Sauropelta had large spines coming out of its shoulders and neck.

Spikes pointing sideways

Gastonia

Gastonia had sharp spikes on its tail. Pairs of spikes opened and closed like scissors and could cut and injure attackers.

Leaf-eaters

Heterodontosaurus

Heterodontosaurus was small and probably ate leaves and roots. It could run very fast to escape from hungry meat-eating dinosaurs.

Long, rough bristles

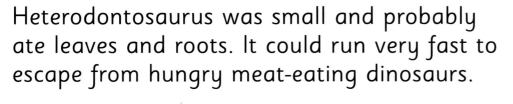

Three long toes on each foot

Claws used to dig in the sand for roots or to tear open insects' nests

Lesothosaurus

Lesothosaurus was not much bigger than a dog. It looked a little like a lizard that could walk on two legs.

Large eyes

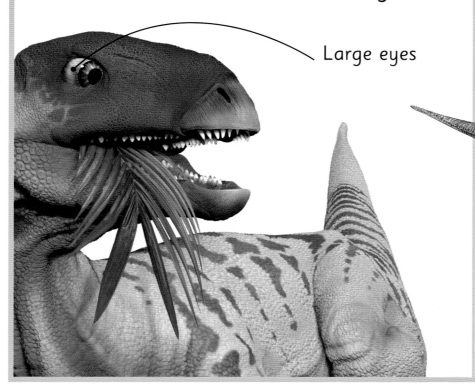

Dryosaurus

Dryosaurus had a turtlelike beak with small teeth, which were used to crush leaves.

Stiff tail

Iguanodon

One of the best-known dinosaurs, Iguanodon was much bigger than many other leaf-eaters. It could probably walk on two legs as well as on all fours.

Toothless beak

Iguanodon skull

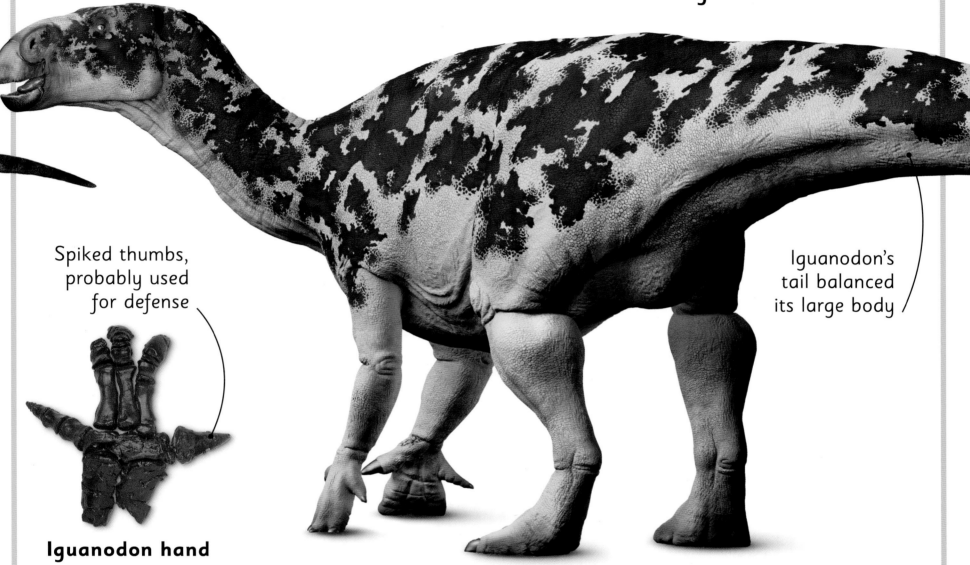

Spiked thumbs, probably used for defense

Iguanodon hand

Iguanodon's tail balanced its large body

Hypsilophodon

Hypsilophodon had big eyes on either side of its head. This gave it an excellent all-around view so it could watch out for danger.

Narrow, sharp beak

Hands with five fingers

Long legs helped Hypsilophodon to run very fast

Duck-billed dinosaurs

Corythosaurus

Corythosaurus means "helmet lizard." It had a thin crest on its head. This was a part of the skull, and it was probably used to attract mates.

Ridge along back

Hollow, bony crest

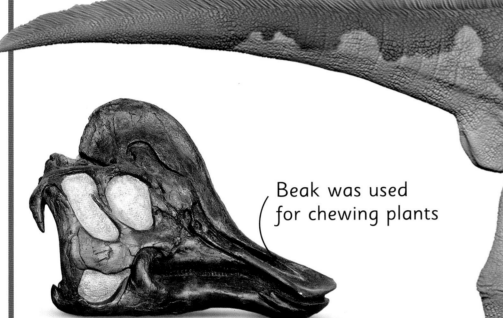

Beak was used for chewing plants

Corythosaurus skull

Gryposaurus

This fossil of Gryposaurus was found in North America. The way the bones fit together show that the tail was held straight out, high off the ground.

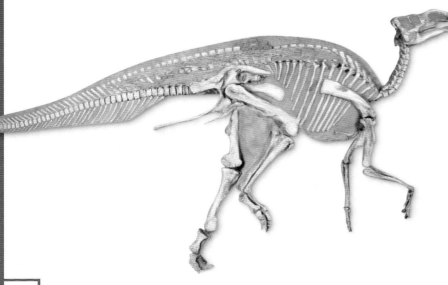

Crest shaped like the blade of an ax

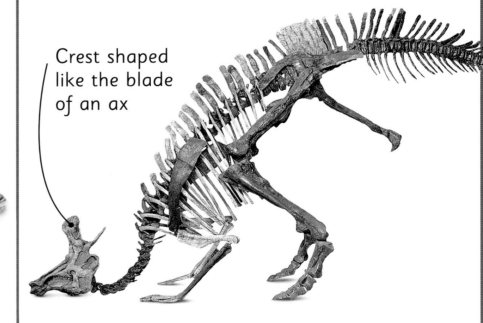

Lambeosaurus

Lambeosaurus had a beak like a duck's, with more than 1,000 teeth used for chewing plants.

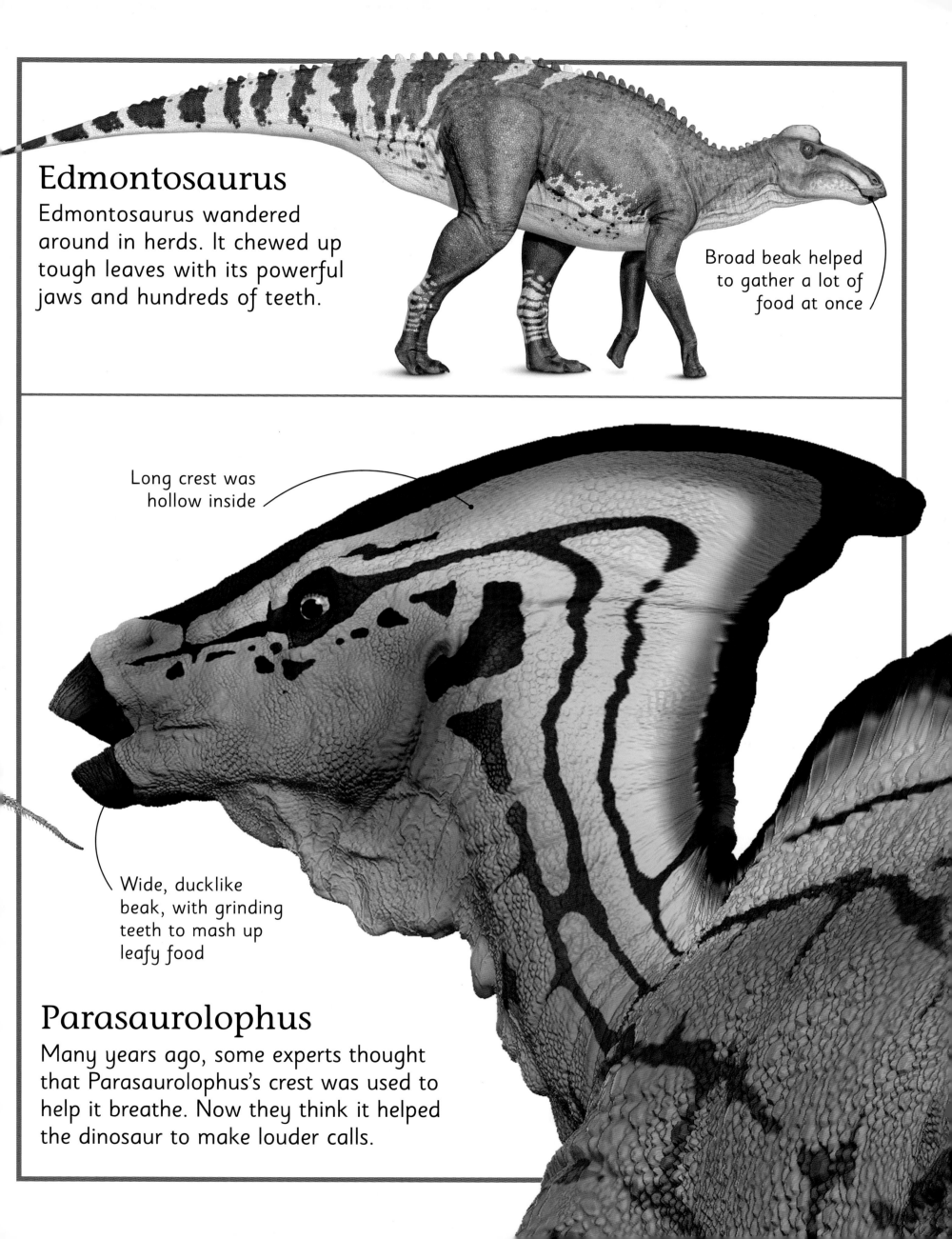

Edmontosaurus

Edmontosaurus wandered around in herds. It chewed up tough leaves with its powerful jaws and hundreds of teeth.

Broad beak helped to gather a lot of food at once

Long crest was hollow inside

Wide, ducklike beak, with grinding teeth to mash up leafy food

Parasaurolophus

Many years ago, some experts thought that Parasaurolophus's crest was used to help it breathe. Now they think it helped the dinosaur to make louder calls.

Boneheads and horns

Styracosaurus

Styracosaurus was a horned-faced dinosaur. It had a head frill with sharp spikes.

Einiosaurus

Einiosaurus had a short frill, with two slim spines growing from the top. This big dinosaur also had a long horn that curved over its snout.

Hooked front horn

Pachycephalosaurus

Pachycephalosaurus had a hard bony head. Experts think these dinosaurs had head-butting contests.

Bony spikes protected the head

Short nose horn

Triceratops

Triceratops was like a huge rhinoceros. This plant-eater used its sharp horns to defend itself against meat-eaters.

Tiny knobs on the head

Stegoceras

Stegoceras had a bony head shaped like an egg. Its narrow snout had tiny teeth that were used to shred and eat leaves.

Head frill

Protoceratops

Protoceratops was the size of a sheep and had a head frill, but no horns. This small dinosaur may have lived in burrows.

Parrotlike beak

Pentaceratops

Pentaceratops means "five-horned face," although this dinosaur had only three horns! There were two on its head and one on its nose. The other two were hornlike growths on its cheeks.

Dinosaur nursery

Nesting together

Dinosaurs laid eggs, as do reptiles and birds. Scientists have found fossils of eggs, nests, and babies belonging to duck-billed dinosaurs called Maiasaura. Female dinosaurs built their nests close together for safety and looked after their babies once the eggs had hatched.

Maiasaura's eggs were pear-shaped and about the size of a child's head

The nests were mounds of soil hollowed out in the middle

Protecting the young

Fossil footprints of the big plant-eaters show that they traveled in herds. The adults protected the younger dinosaurs, as elephants do today with their young.

Meat-eating dinosaur attacking plant-eaters

Young dinosaurs joined herds once they were half as big as adults

Saltasaurus eggs

Saltasaurus eggs were round and the size of small melons. Once these hatched, the tiny babies were probably fed by their parents.

Protoceratops

Protoceratops laid eggs that looked like big potatoes. These were laid in shallow pits made in the sand. The babies were about 8 in (20 cm) long when they hatched.

In scale

Did you spot any of these
dinosaurs earlier in the book?

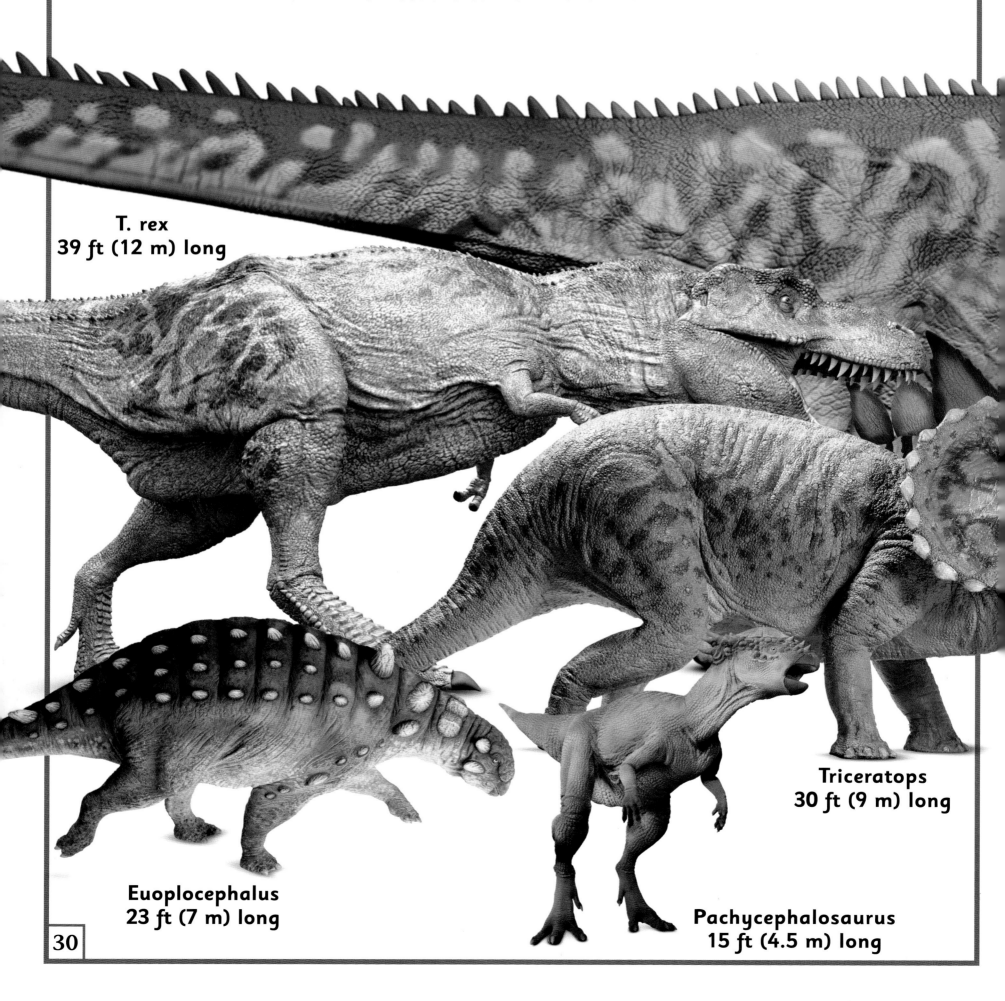

T. rex
39 ft (12 m) long

Triceratops
30 ft (9 m) long

Euoplocephalus
23 ft (7 m) long

Pachycephalosaurus
15 ft (4.5 m) long

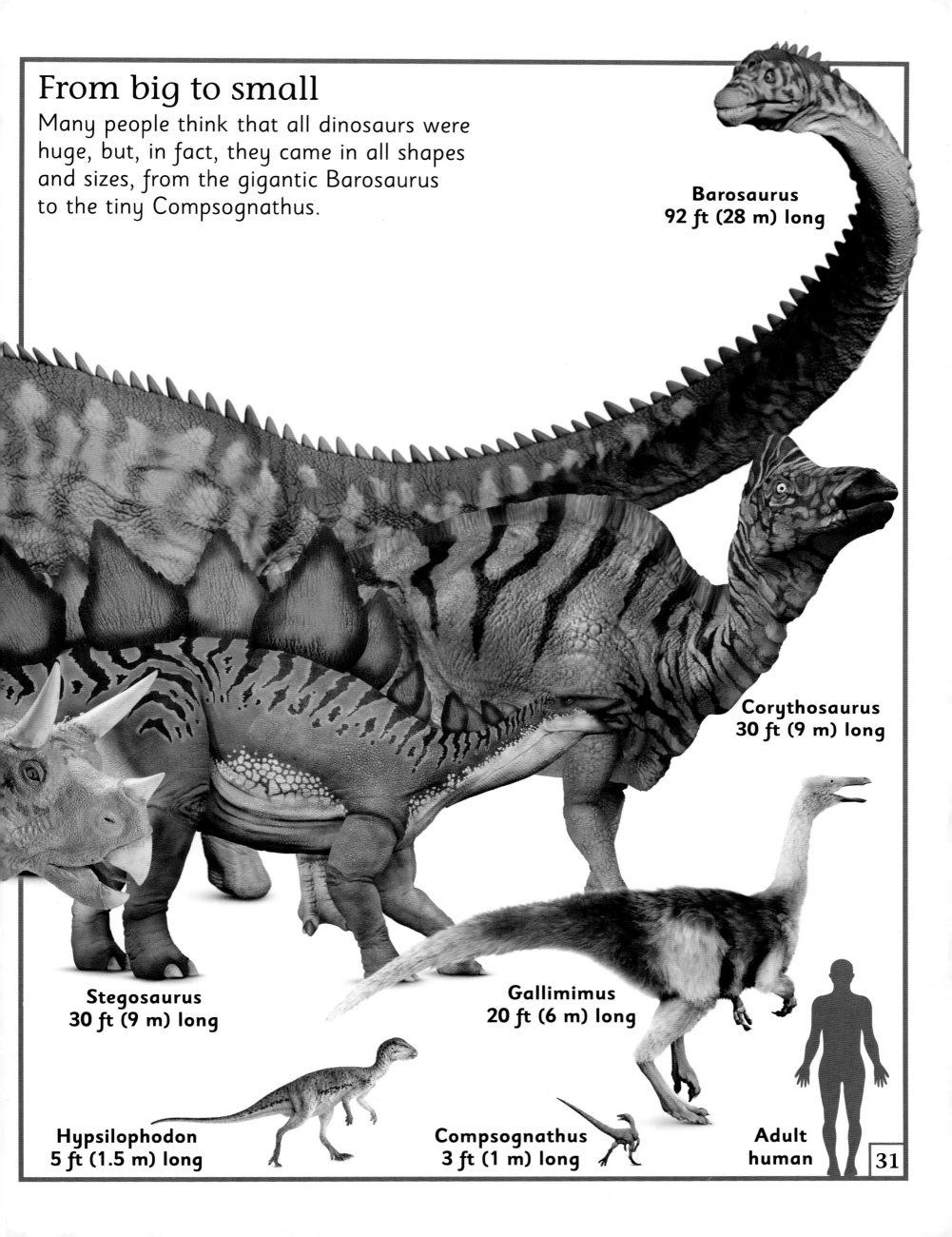

From big to small

Many people think that all dinosaurs were huge, but, in fact, they came in all shapes and sizes, from the gigantic Barosaurus to the tiny Compsognathus.

Barosaurus
92 ft (28 m) long

Corythosaurus
30 ft (9 m) long

Stegosaurus
30 ft (9 m) long

Gallimimus
20 ft (6 m) long

Hypsilophodon
5 ft (1.5 m) long

Compsognathus
3 ft (1 m) long

Adult human

31

Index

Stegosaurus

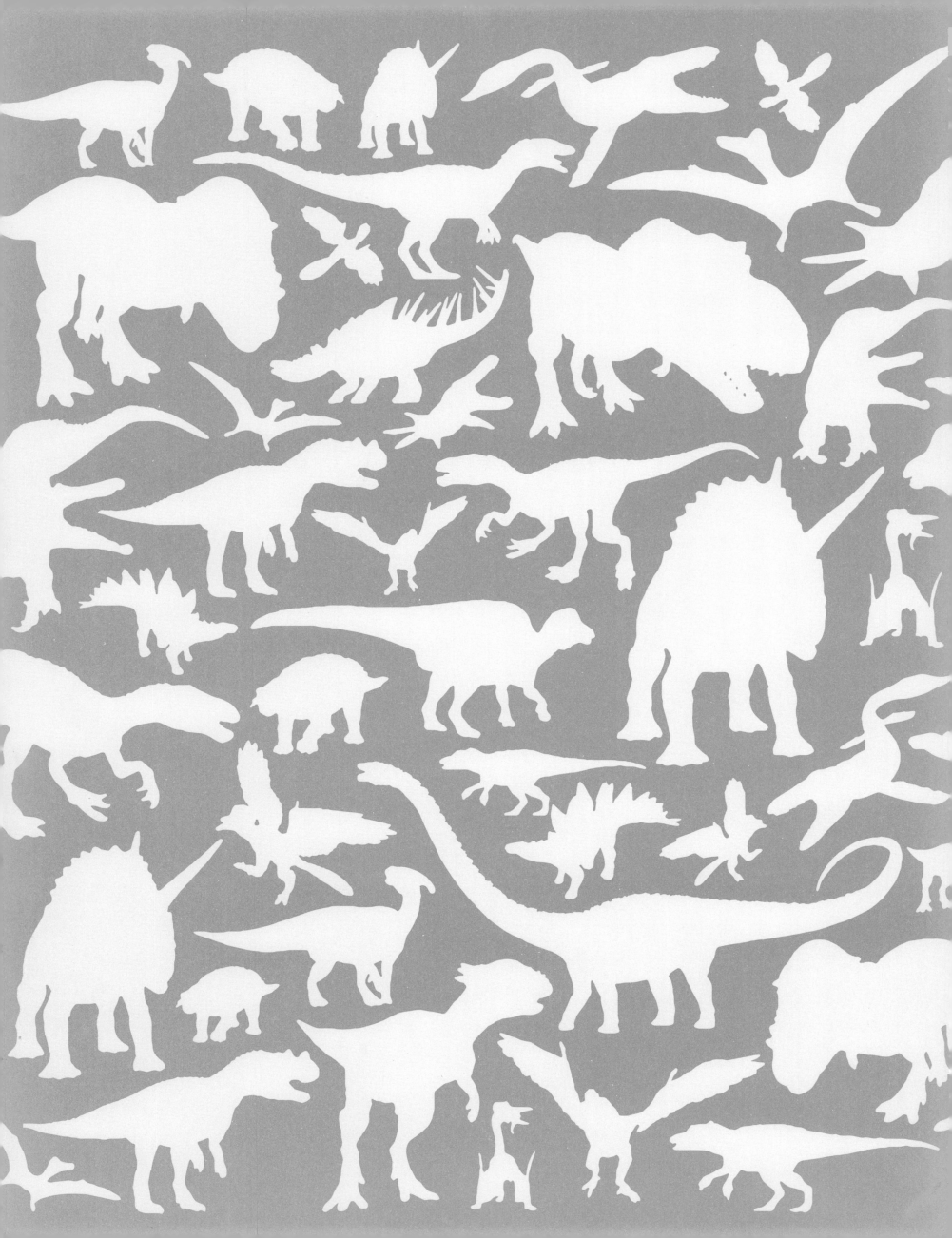